THE COLOR OF HOMEOWNERSHIP:

Increasing Wealth in Black and Brown Communities

By Dr. Tori Brown

The Color of Homeownership:

Increasing Wealth in Black and Brown Communities

Copyright © 2021 by Dr. Tori Brown

All rights reserved. Printed in The United States of America. No part of this publication may be reproduced, stored in a retrieval system or transmitted in any form or by any means electronic, mechanical, photography, copying, recording or otherwise, without prior written permission of the publisher, except in the case of brief quotations embodied in critical articles and reviews. The author rights to "freedom speech' protected by and with the 1st Amendment of the constitution of the United States of America. Books may be purchased for educational, business, or sales promotional use. For information please email successlockdown@gmail.com.

Published in the U.S. by Success Lockdown Group LLC

Located in Tampa Florida

ISBN: 978-1-7351332-3-2 (Print)

ISBN: 978-1-7351332-4-9 (E Book)

Library of Congress Control Number: 2021948762

First Edition

DEDICATION

To my mom Juanita Brown, father John T. Brown, Godmother Ann Jordan, and to all of the future homebuyers that I have not had an opportunity to meet yet. I am looking forward to developing your journey of homeownership, so your family can impact the generations to come.

TABLE OF CONTENTS

Dedication 3

Introduction: 5

Chapter 1: The Haves and the Have Nots 14

Chapter 2: Acid Reflux In Your Pockets 25

Chapter 3: Increasing Homeownership in Black and Brown Communities 38

Chapter 4: Jack and Jill Went Up The Hill 65

Chapter 5: Building an Ark With Homeownership 81

Chapter 6: Situational Generational Poverty Solutions (SGPS) 91

Epilogue: All My Favorite Colors 100

About The Author and Fresh Community Development Inc 110

INTRODUCTION:

The Post Pandemic American Dream

It's almost fall of 2021 and so much has happened since we last spoke. The pandemic has made me lose so many things. I am also in the process of my loss and finding a lot of things as well. In April 2020, right after I started writing the book I published in 2020 called Acid Reflux: How To Stomach This Economy, I lost my Aunt Essie due to Covid. It was so weird and unexpected. My mom's birthday was one week before hers. So being the cute Aries Zodiac sign that they both are of course they called each other to remind each other that it was their birthday. This relationship was very sweet to see, as I watched them each week FaceTime each other often, and reminisce about the olden days when they both were younger.

Well into their 70's I see their strength and wisdom and beauty all wrapped up into one. During this pandemic and their distance FaceTime is how they communicated on a regular basis. I was so proud of my Aunt Essie as I called her because she really knew how to work her IPhone. She was so savvy and creative and just a wealth of wisdom knowledge and scholar of faith and prayer and love for God. She spoke so eloquently as she and mom would laugh on the phone for hours. If you notice, I refer to my Aunt Essie in past tense because yes, Covid claimed her life. While Jesus claimed her soul. It was so fast and unexpected. I mean one week we were all on the IPhone together singing happy birthday to my mom and the next week we were speaking with her to wish her a happy birthday. The very next day she became very ill in the nursing home she lived in and was transported to the hospital a couple days later and a couple days after that she was gone!

Aunt Essie wasn't really my aunt. She was actually an older cousin. But in my family when the older loved one was of age and wisdom, we acknowledge them as an Uncle or an Aunt as a sign of respect to their position in your life. Man...where can we find another acknowledgement or sign of respect as it relates to your position in your life. We are all trying to get there. We want to face it head on so we can identify it as our piece of the pie. Yes you got it, I am talking about The Great American Dream.

This time not only was our dream under attack but our safety is being compromised. Well we know that some have chosen to be vaccinated and others have chosen to not be. There we are with another level of division. See prior to that you know we live in the great divide. Black or white, poor or rich, employed or unemployed, and now vaccinated or unvaccinated. No matter what category you find yourself in there is an even just important divide that we need to talk about and I am going to talk about it right now. Homeowner vs Renter.

Now this can get ugly if you're not prepared to step into the coldness of why some people become homeowners and why some do not. Most can argue that some people choose not to become a homeowner. Others may argue that people don't become homeowners because there is not much help on how to become one. My argument is simple. Information is currency! The point that I make with this argument pivots to this point. The only difference between the haves and the have nots is the information you have access to. Both my argument and point is indicated in the book I wrote last year.

Do you know that we are responsible for what we don't know? Oh you didn't get that life memo. Yes of course, we are. Because now we are living in a world where we are penalized for the things that we do not know. They say that ignorance is no excuse for the law and they mean that! You watch Judge Judy on Television. If they meant that for law then they mean that for you. You have to know stuff, there's no excuse.

You have Google and all these other search engines and books you can use as a reference to become better at anything you want to become better at. What about becoming better at stewardship? What is stewardship? According to Google, stewardship is the job of supervising or taking care of something, such as an organization or property. How can we take care of land we do not own? I remember my dad used to say it was a shame to be 100 years old and don't own a thing with your name on it.

As a kid I didn't understand exactly what he was referring to but I understood ownership is important. Well it is to my family. My father and mom owned their home and their parents both owned their homes as well. So generationally homeownership was just a thing. It's what you did when you became an adult. You owned something as in real estate. It wasn't until I was older and around others that accumulated wealth through asset building strategies that I understood that ownership is what created wealth.

Information is the currency that created the same wealth. So I learned very quickly that the more information I soaked up, the more currency I could create. Let's jump into something right quick, Cryptocurrency. This term became very hot during the pandemic. Especially for those who were studying and participating in it. During the pandemic, I was stuck at home for hours after hours with nothing, but time to read, think, pray, manifest, yes you got it and create currency.

I actually went on a huge vacation for an entire year. I needed that time to heal mentally and physically and spiritually. In this year of peace people say how can you afford to take a year off? Well that's a whole new entire book and I will share it for free on my social media shortly. However, I could vacay the entire year and still make money because of my prior investments and equity positions in other companies that I manage. Most importantly I could take an entire year off and still make money because Information is currency.

One thing I did during the year that was pretty cool and profitable is I invested in stocks and cryptocurrency. I studied where my money was going and why it was going there for that investment. The money I earned in stocks that had decreased during the beginning of the pandemic also rose later on during the pandemic so I was able to take some of those profits from there and drop into the cryptocurrency. If you haven't taken the time to consider cryptocurrency I suggest you follow what I am saying to you. Information is currency and it also becomes cryptocurrency. This book is not about teaching you how to get into cryptocurrency. I will let the gurus tell you all about that. I am just saying I researched it and got into it and just know it's the new wave of how we create currency.

The Post Pandemic American Dream happened right before my eyes. I sold books online at several bookstores. I sold books to friends and family. I was practically selling them out of my trunk like the Rapper Master P. Master P sold his music out of the trunk of his car and today is known as one of the wealthiest Rap Mogul there is today. Well I am no Master P, but I do know the power of information and tried to get this book I had written in 2020 into the hands of thousands of people. Not because I was pushing sales, but only because I was suggesting strategies for people to jump on during the housing market rise. Did you see the news last fall in 2020? Mortgage rates were at an all-time low. People were buying up investment properties everywhere and filling them quickly with renters. Others were also taking advantage of the incentives to purchase their home. That's right, that's where I come in.

As a PHD graduate with a cognate in evaluation and measurement I am a statistician to the heart because I love data. I collect data all of the time and I track it. I tracked my users of special programs and projects and wow did I find out some amazing data. 47 users reported that they used the techniques in my book to purchase a new home. I'm like wait, this is not what I wrote. I wrote with the intention to increase real estate investors, but created a visionary pathway for future homeowners. I even realized a few things as I spoke to these clients.

Homeownership can be a real struggle for people who do not have the tools to become one. I am like no that's not true there are tools. You have realtors and mortgage people and you have HUD. Yes, this is true, but if the target market audience you're speaking to do not have enough information, they may never feel prompted to ever speak to a realtor, mortgage professional, or HUD counselor. Why would they speak to them if they have no reference for homeownership or desire to become a homeowner? Mom or Dad wasn't a homeowner, their parents were not home owners, and before that their parents parent's were not homeowners.

So, generationally we have a history of renters or non-homeowners. Damn! And we wonder why there are barriers to stewardship. We can't beat these people up. We need to normalize homeownership and celebrate the existence of it. The Post Pandemic American Dream is to help increase black and brown homeownership in black and brown communities.

I created a non-profit organization in 2019 with the vision to do just that. Fresh Community Development Group Inc. mission is to provide cost-effective resources to low-income families in need of financial and business literacy to improve their chances for access to housing or home ownership. We are incorporated in Florida, Michigan, and Georgia. Visit us for more information and download the app at www.freshcommunitydevelopment.org.

"You do not have to stay in the rat race of not having".

– ***Dr. Tori Brown***

Chapter 1:

The Haves and the Have Nots

The issue of poverty has impacted the black and brown communities significantly for centuries. The systemic history of poverty didn't start in the last few years. This has been a historical occurrence that has impacted generations and generations dating as far back as the early 1900's and even longer. In 1929 the great depression was one of most historical economical downpours of financial flaw that America had ever seen. The financial flaw was in the inability to protect everyday citizens both black and white from being gravely impacted by the economic tsunami. We can assume because of historical accounts of this, that the African American population of people were at the worst disadvantage for having their needs met during the great depression. In the midst of open racism and discrimination, African American populations experienced severe and extreme financial persecution and fear during.

According to Britannica.com "The Great Depression of the 1930s worsened the already bleak economic situation of African Americans. They were the first to be laid off from their jobs, and they suffered from an unemployment rate two to three times that of whites. In early public assistance programs African Americans often received substantially less aid than whites, and some charitable organizations even excluded Blacks from their soup kitchens." I asked my grandmother who was born in 1918 and was eleven years old at the time what the great depression was like. She recalled that she didn't know when the great depression started and when it ended for her. Prior to 1929 when she was around 4 or 5 years old, she remembered working in the field for picking cotton and butterbeans in the hot and steamy fields of Georgia. The Great Depression wasn't something that started in 1929 and ended in 1930 for her and the family. This was ongoing for years and years to come as she worked from the fields in Georgia all the way up to the Northern State Borders. She learned as a toddler that if they didn't work, they didn't eat.

I often wonder if we have lost that message that was passed on from our loved ones that worked in the fields of the Deep South. Do we understand that at any given time we could be placed in a position of situational poverty? What is situational poverty? Situational Poverty, according to Google, is caused by a sudden crisis or loss that is often temporary and can be resolved with a few tools and strategies in place. Situational poverty occurs when there is a lack of resources due to a particular event. We have seen a lot of situations in these last few months where resources that were there for the pandemic are starting to dry up. I am referring to unemployment benefits being cut and the housing moratorium being lifted that has been creating mass evictions across the state.

Some have argued that the unemployment benefits were providing more income than actual employers therefore people did not want to return to work. The argument of others is the shame that people are working for such low wages in the first place to the point that the help that they are receiving has been more beneficial than the actual employment. My argument is no matter which argument you agree on or not, people are still in poverty and living below their means and this is impacting the children more than anything. Growing up in poverty is never an ideal experience for a growing young mind that needs food, water, shelter, protection, education, and clothes to survive in this ever changing economy and world.

I remember when a good friend of mine was facing eviction from her apartment. It was the type of situation that would bring tears to my eyes every time. It hurts so much to see the people you love struggle financially. I remember her attempts to borrow gas money to drive to the food pantry so the children can eat. She never blinked an eye when it came to surviving for her and those kids. She did what she had to do to survive and sometimes it just wasn't good enough. It's emotionally taxing to struggle financially year after year after year after year. The facts are in her case the struggle didn't just start with her. Her struggle came from a place of the generational financial struggle. Her mom had the same struggles as she did at her age. Her grandmother had a similar struggle with financial problems. This is what we call generational poverty.

According to Google, generational poverty occurs in families where at least two generations have been born into poverty. In these cases of generational poverty, the financial struggle has been normalized. Having financial issues is expected and their strategy to deal with it is to keep "doing the best they can." I actually hate those words when I see people that I love struggle. I hate it because deep down inside I know that they really truly mean that and they truly don't know what to do about it. They take what they can get and they accept that the struggle will always be part of their life. I just want to say in a heartfelt moment that this statement does not have to always be true.

That is why I really work so hard to spread the information I have about entrepreneurship. I know from personal experiences that becoming a business owner of something is better than becoming an employee of nothing. If they can't hire you, be sure to hire yourself. If they can't feed you, learn how to feed yourself. Remember in the early sharecropping days my grandmothers and grandfathers did not have a choice. If they did not work they did not eat. If they did not kill something they did not eat. They prepared livestock and crops to sell and eat to live off the land. But in order to do that they had to own something. They had to own the land they lived on and they had to own the crops they picked, they had to own the livestock they killed to eat every night. No one was going to give them anything.

My grandfather John Brown self-taught himself how to plant different crops and build a smokehouse so he could sell his specialty to the community to get himself out of debt and his sharecropping agreement. Not only was that savvy and strategic, but it was a go hard or go home move we would refer to it as today. My grandfather went hard to take his special skills into the marketplace to increase his chances of owning more land and repeating the process for good stewardship. If you read my book Acid Reflux you will know that I wrote a chapter called The Haves and the Have Nots. Here is a question for you to think about. Was my grandfather a Have or a Have not?

I bring up this question because I am reminded that my brother Ty after reading my book asked me that. He says, "Hey sis, am I a Have or a Have not?". That was a great question with a lot of weight on it. What is a have versus a have not? Well as i have explained many times before, the only difference between the Haves and the Have nots is the information you have access to. Did my grandfather have access to information? Yes he did. He used a lot of instinct and prayer as my Aunt Sallie would say as she referred to my grandfather as Papa. I never met Papa, but the stories I heard about him assured me that I have a lot of Papa in me in how I strategize and process information and put them into action.

I'm not sure if it was the farmers' almanac or asking other farmers or experimenting with different crops to grow specialized fruits and vegetables for a profit, I don't know. What I do know is that Papa had a family to feed and he was determined to figure it out. What would make Papa in this case be a Have Not? I guess if he received all of this information and he didn't apply it to create currency then he would put himself in a position to be a Have not. Papa didn't have Google like we do today to look up information and communicate to the other end of the world for consumer goods to sell. What are consumer goods? If you didn't read my last book I'm going to give a cheat note. Consumer goods are things that you go into debt for only for the purpose of creating income with that good to create revenue. Why are we not using more consumer good techniques and strategies to increase our access to wealth? Well remember generationally you are prone to repeat the same strategies and adaptations that you learned from your parents of guardian figures.

If all you know how to do is hustle because your parents were hustlers then you learn how to hustle. I don't knock the hustle now because I learned the hustle from my dad. I just had to take that hustle mentality and turn it into something that was going to expand and scale in the format of a legitimate business endeavor. Now don't go trying to guess what my Papa's hustle was. I will cover that one day in another book. Let's just stay with the idea that the things that your parents do good, bad, or indifferent can be passed down to you and it's your job to determine if these are the things that add to your road to financial success and ownership or does it take away from it.

Generational poverty, let's go back to it. When I asked my mom about her access to homeownership and why did she do it her answer was simple. I did it for my family. She recalled the day she made up her mind to pursue homeownership with my dad. She says that I was a baby in the crib only a few months old and learning to hold my milk bottle. She noticed while I was holding my bottle that there were roaches crawling all over my baby crib. Now she knew we had roaches in the house however, she was appalled that those critters would crawl in my crib while she was having a proud moment to hold my bottle on my own. That was the last straw, she told my father that's it! We are buying a house. He agreed and they went looking for a home that was purchased. She said there were no hesitations to leave that rental. She knew that with her own home she could take care of it better than the old apartment she tried so hard to clean and fix up as much as they could when the landlord was not responding to their immediate need for maintenance.

I can tell you that I grew up in a single income household. My dad worked the 3rd shift in a foundry. His dad provided a single income household as well. They made it work. That generation I come from strategizes to make it work. I make a living today because I provide strategies for people in need of services for options to make it work for them. It's my contribution to aiding the thousands of people that I have worked with over the years making sure that they break generational and situational poverty. My life's work has been based around giving information and helping others achieve their American Dream and how ever they dream it.

On this new mission I am determined to create more homeowners. I don't want people caught up in poverty. I want people to break the mindset that creates poverty. Poverty starts in your mind long before it hits your pockets. This mindset comes from the thoughts that "I'm doing the best I can". Yes and No. The best you can do is that you tried to pick up on the information to create the currency and someone didn't allow you to access the information. It's up to you to do something with the information you have access to. There are so many tools out here to help you break the chains of poverty, but you have to first identify that you are in poverty.

It's so easy to get on social media and show the people you're rich because you rented a hotel room or a fancy car. Let's be real, that is what they call "frontin for the gram." Why do people do that? Well it has a lot to do with wanting a lifestyle that they really can't afford. News flash, getting access to credit cards with high limits so you can blow money like you hit the lotto is not rich. It's just plain irresponsible and shows just how fiscally unfit a person is with the handling of money. Access to money is not the real currency. Access to information that creates the currency is the real money here. If you can't receive information, then it becomes difficult to produce currency.

Sad to say that a financial recession is still set to come and I am still on a journey to help people build their financial ark. I am providing you with the information so you do not have to live generationally as a Have Not.

My friend here in the story by the way broke the generational poverty. She is a business owner and currently owns a few properties that she rents out to other mothers just like her looking to pivot during a bout with situational poverty. She learned how to help people improve their credit and as a service she does this for renters. Let's normalize providing strategies for people we know and love. If we just keep giving them money they will never learn how to get out of their situation. I may have helped her out here and there but the biggest gift I taught her was entrepreneurship. If I would have given her the fish she would have eaten for the day. But I taught her how to fish and now she can eat forever. She never needed me to ever be her crutch, she needed me to be strong and supportive enough to say No to giving handouts but absolutely yes to giving hands Up!

"Poverty starts in your mind long before it hits your pockets".

– Dr. Tori Brown

Chapter 2:

Acid Reflux In Your Pockets

Wait a minute! "Shut the front door" as my good friend Tiffany says when there is some shocking information to process and think about. I was reading today that some states are asking that the people that received unemployment benefits pay the money back. Okay I am confused for a minute or two. Has anybody ever been able to squeeze water from a rock? I'm just asking for a friend. Okay you got me...I am the friend that's asking! What in the John Brown are we doing these days? I mean was there some fine print that the people that received the unemployment didn't see. Like wow this is hard! Acid Reflux in Your Pockets people. We have to bring some solutions to the people. In emergency situations, the paramedics come to stop the bleeding in the wound victim. Okay so if this isn't a wound that is bleeding I don't know what else is.

So let's quickly talk about how to control the bleeding. If you or someone you love or know is in a situation like this and needs immediate help please contact your local credit consultant. I am serious. Work on your credit or pay someone to work on your credit. I am talking about minimizing your current debts. I am talking about curving your appetite to eat out so much and social spend and splurge. Now I realize this is not the issue with everyone in this situation, but for most people it's about prioritizing your spending and looking for ways to increase your income. I am talking about turning off your video games, stop scrolling your social media page for emotional entertainment and pleasure. I'm talking about getting you a book with some strategies that will help you solve and minimize some of your financial struggles. It's simple math for those that are ready to apply it. Spend NOTHING and earn EVERYTHING. I mean it, do it! Treat the Acid Reflux in your pockets like it is really acid and it is harmful if not treated.

When I was a kid and my mom would give me a crispy $50 dollar bill she would tell me, "Don't let it burn a hole in my pocket." What does she mean by that statement? She was warning me to save my money and do not spend it on just anything. I learned early on not to let money "burn a hole in my pocket." Sometimes I treat money and finances as if I don't have it. I build asset wealth yearly as a good financial advisor told me to do years ago. She told me it was wise to build assets yearly while spending less discretionary funds each month.

What are discretionary funds? Money that I use to do whatever I want. I actually operate opposite of people that get access to money.

Looking rich is not what is important to me. Feeling good about the financial choices I make and taking the time off when I need to do it is what's more important. Don't get me wrong, I love going out of town and traveling to sight see and experience the land, but right now in this last year I have really wanted to stay in and really focus on what is important to me. Providing tools and information is very important to me. The work my non-profit is doing to help others become homeowners is important to me. This task is so important that I am going to give you some tools to get the Acid Reflux Out Your Pockets.

What is Acid Reflux In Your pockets? Well I am so glad you asked. 1.) It's when you have grown accustomed to chasing money and that money chase has created a habit that is causing you stress and illness. My mentor Henry "Coach" Washington taught me this a long time ago. He said stop chasing money and let that money catch up with you. Chasing money is exhausting, and it is addictive. When you're addicted to getting money, you can find yourself doing anything to get it such as PPP fraud and other stuff that I won't go into depth here. Money is a tool, and you should treat it like such. It's not a way to control the person you say you love or to gain access to the big boy club, it's a resource tool to help you gain access. That's really all you need is access. Remember the only difference between the have and the have nots is the information you have access to.

That money can give you access and open doors for the opportunity to experience the best life. You just have to put some things into perspective so you can conserve for a rainy day. Use the money to build asset wealth. I talk a lot about asset wealth. What is it? It comes from the term wealth asset in which it can be interchangeably used. According to Google, wealth asset is described as the Wealth measures of value of all the assets of worth owned by a person, community, company, or country. Wealth is determined by taking the total market value of all physical and intangible assets owned, then subtracting all debts. Essentially, wealth is the accumulation of scarce resources. What's scarce and what's not scarce? Simple math everyone, information. Information is data and its accumulative and though it can be speculative at times, it still is abundant and available for you to convert into currency.

What is Acid Reflux In Your pockets? 2.) It is the greed that comes from a place of lack and psychologically is present in people with low emotional intelligence. I have studied some research in emotional intelligence as it relates to consumer spending. Research supports that people with lower emotional intelligence measurements have a higher interest in frivolous spending. Let's talk about it. Emotional Intelligence (EI) is the ability to perceive, control, and evaluate emotions and is often referred to as EI. When you encounter someone with high emotional intelligence you may not notice this as an attribute or characteristic in the persona you interact with on a daily basis. However, if you find yourself around someone with a lower emotional intelligence feature you may notice it right away.

In fact, you may not be able to identify that it's there, but your abrasive engagement with them can be most noticed by their behaviors. Remember, someone with low EI may appear selfish, self-centered, and very difficult to get along with. Someone with low emotional intelligence will have emotional outbursts, become very abrasive and unfeeling, they always have to be right in circumstances, very oblivious to other people's feelings, have poor coping skills, and often blame others for their problems. Emotional Intelligence is something different from Intelligence Quotients which is known as IQ. EI is something that can be increased through skill building and development. IQ is not something you can increase or develop, you either have a higher IQ or you don't. Emotional Intelligence is something that can be increased through various treatment modalities and professional development techniques. When you have a relationship with your money that comes from a place of greed, you will often find that your intent for acquiring more of it is just continuing to feed your appetite for more and more of it. There is nothing wrong with wanting to acquire wealth and resources.

It is just often greed can sometimes cloud your judgement for how you go about obtaining it. This may include making bad choices with severe consequences such as committing PPP Fraud. In order to make sure you are not putting yourself in financial and emotional harm, it is important that you self-reflect and evaluate why you want to obtain wealth and what you plan to do with the wealth you desire to have. This is why it is extremely important that you practice self-evaluation often in your lifestyle so you can increase your Financial Emotional Intelligence. Financial emotional intelligence is understanding what we feel about money and why. It is really zeroing in on what money means to us emotionally, so we can feelingly welcome more money into our lives and enjoy it. Everyone wants to feel good and most believe that having access to a surplus of money will make you feel the best.

Now some may argue that money is not everything while others may argue that those people just have not yet had enough money yet to change that belief. I believe that money is a tool for access to opportunity and resources that can create multiple roads to achieving personal success, but that's just me and my perception and my relationship with money. My personal belief system is tied to my interest in building strong families and communities. Therefore, my time which converts to money in conjunction with my information which also converts to money (Thus, my mantra that information is currency) is well spent and invested in the tools I provide to families and communities that are interested in developing wealth assets.

So again, what is acid reflux in your pockets? 3.) It is frivolous spending and buying things that you do not absolutely need. We all want to feel good and we all want to vibe with the YOLO (You Only Live Once) theme because it feels good to say. However, while you are living life once, it's so important to think through the course of what you want this life you're living to look like and set a plan to live it effectively. Last year I was being interviewed for a magazine article and the young lady that was interviewing me asked me about the title in my bio that I use. I refer to myself as a Lifestyle Engineer. Why did I call myself a Lifestyle Engineer? Well why not, I am a licensed psychologist and have practiced therapeutic modalities with several clients and families over the years in which I practice.

Out of all of the work in my past role as a clinical therapist, I'm most proud of how I made sure it was important that my clients understood that I valued them as a person. When you are in the field of therapy, it is so easy to get burnt out. I mean in most settings you could easily be providing treatment for 40 to 60+ people a week. How is that possible right? Well you have individual and group therapy in which you are responsible for people's lives. I remember speaking with an airplane pilot and we were both talking of our professions and the pros and cons of the work. I asked him how he deals with the pressure of having so many lives in his hands as he is navigating a large plane to land on a small landing strip over the water when flying into the Washington DC airport. He says oh that's easy for me. He jokingly said he would be more afraid of having people live in his hands week after week with therapy sessions. From that moment on I had real pressure because he was right. That is a lot to become responsible for.

As therapists we are responsible for making sure that we bring our full self as a professional to our therapeutic session as my mentor and professor Dr. Yvonne Calloway would tell us. She even told me often as I would recant wanting to things that I should have done different in different therapeutic settings. She would lovingly and jokingly tell me to "stop should-ing" on myself and she was right. You can't "should" your way out of stuff so as a trained therapist for moving people through the therapeutic process to progress, my background prepared me to become that Lifestyle Engineer people need to also tell them to stop "should-ing" on yourself and create the lifestyle you want that includes good emotional intelligence and use of great Emotional Financial Intelligence.

Frivolous spending is a sign that you have not yet set any financial goals and do not have the intentions to ever become strengthened in building wealth assets. It is one thing to not know better, but it's something else to know better, but do not have the motives to want to do better. Making excuses for your behaviors in spending is a form of avoidance from the idea that you may not truly believe that you deserve something of value that resembles wealth. You have to ask yourself the hard questions. Do you want to build wealth? Maybe you really don't and perhaps you see items such as buying a home just as another goal and not a means to get to a goal. Homeownership gives you a display for achieving a successful lifestyle. It's something about ownership that should make you want to take pride in how you live. When you own something you should take care of it better. Some may not because they do not value the access that ownership brings you in building your wealth asset.

I have known people who own a home that has not taken any time to do anything to maintain the upkeep of the property. The clutter in their home space may be a simular representation of the clutter in their mind and that's okay for them, but for you my friend you are reading because I assume you want more so I get to share more with you. I get to tell you more, I get to push you more and challenge you more to think about what you do financially and why you are doing it. If you find yourself frivolous spending frivolously, then you will find yourself doing some of the things I mentioned above like chasing money and being greedy with money. These are all the characteristics that you may have Acid Reflux in your pockets that can be harmful to both your financial, mental, and physical health. Going forward making sure you are able to identify what is causing the illnesses is just as important as understanding that you have an illness when it comes to your financial health. This brings me to my last point of uncovering.

What is Acid Reflux In Your pockets? 4.) It is not setting goals for asset wealth for you and your family. This one is not as complicated as the previous three because it's straight and to the point. Ask yourself this and be honest about your answer. Are you a Have or a Have not? If you are part of the haves, then you're free to go. Class is closed and session has concluded. You are part of the 1% of people in this world like

Warren Buffet, Jeff Bezos, and Elon Musk etc. Most recently Jeff Bezos gifted a few select people with 100 Million Dollars to do what they see fit to do with the dollars. One of the people selected is Van Jones, CNN news contributor. Now some may argue that he only donated it for tax purposes. No matter what his reason for doing it was, the point is Mr Bezos had the capital to do it. That capital can be used in many ways to create life changing differences in people's lives around the world. Remember this same world involves people that don't have much of anything. So the next time you want to purchase your 20th Rolex because you are part of the Haves hopefully on a humanitarian perspective you can remember that the cost of that Rolex could have created housing for lots of children and family.

I am not saying that you should not have nice things. I own nice things. However, I am just asking to consider the people around you that are looking at hope because they can't see Jeff Bezos but they can see you everyday. They can talk to you everyday. They can experience what you experience and gain hope because you gave them that picture of hope in how you handle your money. If you are a have not and want to become on the team of the Haves then you have to put some things in perspective. One of the main perspectives you need to have is making sure you are setting goals for asset wealth.

Do you ever see yourself owning 5 to 6 homes? The more asset wealth you build the more flexible of a lifestyle that you can obtain. I am not here to tell you that you should acquire 5 or 6 homes. I am here to encourage you that you CAN acquire 5 or 6 homes and use them as assets. It's not impossible. It's just a process in which you are welcome to obtain.

The main foundational thing to know about the acquiring of asset wealth is that this begins with the purchase of your first house. Homeownership is the stepping stone for closing the wealth gap between black and whit families. Leaving legacy and assets with great knowledge nuggets is how you live forever and this my friend is your true escape to YOLO. Living once requires that you have done what you needed to do for yourself and your family while you were here. Acid Reflux in your pocket is harmful and can be prevented. You just have to be honest with yourself about what you want for your lifestyle, how you want to get it, and what are your plans for achieving it.

"Homeownership is one of the most important factors in decreasing the wealth gap we see between black and white populations. When we increase ownership we increase wealth for black and brown families in our communities".

– Dr. Tori Brown

Chapter 3:

Increasing Homeownership in Black and Brown Communities

According to the 2021 U.S. In 2020 we saw a decline in the purchase of new housing and homeownership. However, in 2021 despite it being publicized as an increased housing market; research by the U.S. Census Bureau shows that there was a significant decline in the purchase of housing. So who exactly benefited from the housing market boom other than the real estate investors? The market did indeed increase the number of purchases of real estate investment property. But how exactly did these real estate investors' purchases benefit the families that live in them? It didn't. It only placed them in a position of accessing housing not The Ownership of that house. If you haven't noticed, everyone is talking about affordable housing in 2021. You have different celebrities releasing apps and purchasing land and really getting involved in the trend of affordable housing.

My sister is a realtor and she told me that Zillow now owns houses. I thought that made a lot of business strategy sense. I mean why not, they are one of the largest search engines for houses and it's just about a household name such as Google and Geico. Nothing stays the same in a moving economy and that does include the prices of major purchases like housing. In March of 2020 I started the development of building a new house from the ground up for my mom. By the time the house was built in December, the comps on the house had increased significantly and the interest rates were nice and low for 750+ credit scores. In fact, clients in 2021 were buying several properties unlike my clients in 2020. These clients were getting ready to capitalize off of the housing market and increased rent rates. Some clients rented their properties, some purchased to renovate and sale known as fix and flip, while some purchased property to Airbnb out that typically yields 3 times the profit that rent rows does (Rent Rows is referred to the property you rent out and the income that comes to the landlord as profit from that renter).

Something interesting happened to my clients that read the book Acid Reflux. The intended audience was for the real estate investor clients that were trying to get into investing in properties and building assets. Clients that read the book became first time homebuyers and then turned around and became landlords through the purchase of investment properties. This is what I call excitement. Imagine making a pot of soup and then realize that this pot of soup becomes the main meal. This is what we call cooking with grease. So as I backtracked the book and information in the book it dawned on me that I gave strategies that not only can increase wealth assets but increase homeownership as well. So, how do we increase homeownership in black and brown communities? Elementary my dear watson as Sherlock Holmes with say. It is exactly just unlocking and uncovering the puzzle pieces. Here are the steps for black and brown to consider when purchasing a home.

Questions to consider:

- If you had the opportunity would you purchase a home?
- Where would you purchase this home?
- How much of a home could you afford?

I can tell you from experience it's a challenge to do something that has never been done before. When I say never been done before I mean that YOU have never done it before. That does not mean that it can't be done first by you. There have been a lot of experiences in my life in which I had to go first. In my early education in middle school I was the first to be accepted at a school for the gifted. I was the first documented entrepreneur in my family. I was the first with a doctorate degree from a University in my family. I was even the first generation college student in the family. My time at Eastern Michigan University I became the first in the family to step into a clinical program that required that I bring my full self to the work. I remember my training as a clinician in my first graduate program. This was the first time I had ever experienced having a secretary to check in with regarding the scheduling of my appointments. It's a challenge and definitely something new when you have to operate and communicate with someone to coordinate your schedule. I was too nervous to feel important and confident about having a secretary or receptionist. I was timid and scared inside and really not sure of myself.

My exterior looked as if I had it all together but my interior was anxious and unsure. When I was first introduced to Stephany the receptionist, I instantly realized it was something different about her. She too was a young African American woman so instantly it seemed as if I had someone that looked like me that I could relate to in that clinical department. She was pleasant, friendly, helpful, and very knowledgeable about the entire department. I really began to notice how she went above and beyond to assist me as I fumbled through trying to fit in socially within a predominantly white and white male dominated work environment.

It was training but believe me it was work learning how to put on psychological capes to help clients work through their life issues in therapy. After one evening of completing a client session I was able to talk with Stephany one on one without inhibitions. As we spoke casually about our environment we realized that we were both from the same hometown of Saginaw Michigan. We were both absolutely floored to find out that we both came from Saginaw and we both escaped the negative environment of Saginaw to come to Ypsilanti Michigan in search of a better life and lifestyle. It really felt good having someone that could relate to your past and see your attempts to move toward your future. This became the friendship that extended beyond that day. I laugh with her often about how far we have come.

I knew it was something special about her. She wasn't just a receptionist or secretary, she was a force and powerhouse under this poised and graceful smile she wore every day. She was educated and a chief executive officer (CEO) in the making and she knew how to hide all of that behind her meek and humble personality. Well as we say in Saginaw, "game recognize, game", because she saw the same attributes in me. We both knew back then that we were capable of doing so much more than what we were doing. Over the years we have been able to successfully do so, but the heartbeat of that situation is identifying someone in your life that will always inspire you to do better. I remember when she inspired me to purchase my first house. I had the opportunity to purchase but was not quite sure if I wanted to. The main reason for not being sure was, I was scared. Honestly, I didn't know if I could afford it. I also didn't know where to purchase it. At the time I was living in downtown Detroit but I worked 30 minutes away in Monroe Michigan. Monroe Michigan was a very small town just north of Toledo Ohio. It was a predominantly white town with often chatter about racial divide and racism.

I knew this first hand because working there every day I saw the environment of that community. Knowing the community and loving the community became one in the same because I made connections and friends with both black and white residents and professionals in that county. That still did not make me hesitate to want to live in that community. It just so happens that my favorite builder was building there; and yes I do have a favorite builders list like some people have favorite NFL and NBA teams. One day I stopped in and met with the sales agent and she showed me different designs they were building in that community. I had the opportunity to design my new home from the ground to the ceiling. However, I was willing to pass that opportunity up until I ran it by Stephany. Boy, what did I do other than tell this cheerleader my fears and she knocked them all down one by one. It didn't help that she had experience in homeownership and mortgages. She taught me that buying a home now was equivalent to building a financial future. I tell you, you have to trust anyone named Stephany that spells their name with a Y at the end. They will never steer you wrong. The next thing I remember we were calculating how much of a house I could afford. The rest is in the history books after I purchased my first home.

Here I was in my early 20's and making my first home purchase. To be honest I really didn't understand what I was getting myself into. The only thing I knew is I qualified and had the opportunity to buy it and I did it. Sometimes it takes situations in which people will get presented with opportunities to do something like purchase a home. When I think back in my relationships and friendships I was one of the few that were purchasing a home. It wasn't as if purchasing a home was an everyday topic with me and my friends. The opportunity to purchase my first home just sort of "fell into my lap", as they say. I am encouraging you to think about taking advantage of any and every opportunity there is to obtain homeownership.

More questions to consider:

- Do you have consistent income for at least 2 years?

- Have you filed your last two tax returns?
- Have you pulled your credit in the last 30 days?
- Do you have derogatory information on your credit profile?

There are many things that you need to be thinking about if you are planning to purchase a new house within the next 12-15 months. These questions to consider are just the next level from the above questions that you would ask yourself and answer it in the most honest way possible. As mentioned before homeownership is not a hocus pocus quick game hustle with an overnight result. You have to understand that purchasing a home is a major purchase and requires that you cross all the T's and dot all the I's prior to the process. The questions above are things you consider answering honestly on your own before you speak to a real estate agent. These questions are the things you ask yourself before you speak to a mortgage or banker regarding the lending process.

If you have worked at the same job for two or more years with consistent income, this is going to be the minimum requirement. Some will require more years. It also looks favorable on your end if you have worked in the same employment industry for three to four years. If your income is derived from self-employment, it's important that you have consistent income for at least three to four years. This will include allowing the lender to see bank statements for each year of your business over the past four years. One may wonder why they will need all of this information. Let's consider this scenario if you were the lender. For example let's say that you have an extra $240,000 laying around and someone wants to borrow all of it to purchase a house.

In this case you will absolutely want to know everything about that person you just met that wants to borrow that amount from you. Would it make a difference to you if the person worked at the same job for seven years or if the person only worked for himself for a year? I believe the practical choice would be to lend to the person who has a good working history with good pay from the last seven years. Chances are he will be able to pay you back for that debt. Would you trust the person with the self-employment making money here and there for the past year? Yeah I wouldn't either. So the point that I am making here is you have to look lendable to the lender especially when it comes to your income.

No one wants to lend money to a homeowner to purchase it, if they have the potential to lose it later. The truth is, in some cases of predatory lending they will lend to you for that purpose. It's sad to say this but, in the past, and maybe still in the current, lenders have been allowed to lend to people subprime because they know that the PMI would pay the insurance for losing the house. Subprime is lending to a group of people that have the minimum credit score under 620 to qualify for a house. A subprime credit score would be 540. Your credit score determines your history for lending and should be above 700 for best interest rates. Some indicators that tend to show that the housing market could soon tank is the amount of predatory lenders that approved houses to people they knew would not be able to keep up the payments to their house. This was especially a challenge for homeowners that purchased a home with a ARM vs a Fixed Rate.

Filing your tax returns is very important to have prior to that start of exploring the purchase of a home. Your taxes tell the lender everything they need to know in order to suggest approval or denial for a mortgage loan. I recommend that you use a professional tax preparer when submitting tax returns to your lender for review. This is the case especially for those who are self-employed. Unless you have experience with filing tax returns I recommend that you leave that job to the professionals who know the current tax laws to help you. Sometimes when you just use a software online you may miss out on human eyes that can manually make sense of your credit report filing and in cases in which your lender needs an explanation your CPA or Tax Preparer can provide you with one. The taxes are just one part of the footwork you need to do as preparation for the house purchase.

The credit score is a very important factor. As mentioned above your credit score determines your loan interest rate. It's helpful to have almost an 800+ credit score to qualify for the absolute best rates. If you do not have 800+ then you need to make sure you are applying for 700+. Anything below 620 FICO and could become prime and minimize your chances of affording the actual house because they will add on what they call PMI on a loan. According to Google, PMI is also known as Private Mortgage Insurance and is a type of mortgage insurance you might be required to pay for if you have a conventional loan. PMI is a type of insurance that will pay the lender back in event that the lender defaults on the loan. This works just as if you purchase a cell phone and lose it, take out an insurance claim, and someone sends you a check for the replacement.

This is all the concept except if you lose your house for non-payment, the lender wins the amount of money borrowed from the house from the insurance and someone else gets a paid house that they will resell and put back on the market. This information I am sharing with you is not intended to make you angry and resentful of the process. My attempt is to prepare you for the process of getting ready for the purchase of your new home. The credit score is important. Guard it with your life especially because it is your life. You can't get anything done if you take four steps forward and one step back. You have to prioritize your spending. Almost never apply for a bunch of credit cards and then purchase a house. You will increase your debt to income ratio that should be below 43%. This typically includes your student loans.

Do not be afraid to look at your credit asap. You do not want to be surprised with the realtor when your pre-approval is declined, that's embarrassing. I am trying to show you realistically what you can do prior to calling the realtor or mortgage person, pull your credit from the last 30 days. If you have derogatory information on your credit report be sure to work with certified credit consultants or work towards credit consulting certification, either way you have to learn how to read your credit report and how to increase your credit scores.

Additional Questions:

- Have you saved up any money for a down payment?
- Are you willing to increase your income?
- Do you have any social support from friends and family in purchasing a home?

These additional questions may not be as important as the first two sets of questions, however, they should be taken seriously in this chapter. Everything that I am taking on to take the time to write in this book is created with the full intent to make sure you win. Some people are just making it day by day while others are out here winning every day. I know from experience that it takes a village of winners to raise up another winner. I also know that not everyone has that support of a winning team around them. Sometimes people have to learn how to get on track to living a lifestyle that is often seen on television and social media. As I look at my social media contacts, I review how they are living their life and playing it out before their audiences. Many of the social media influencers are making a living off of selling the products that teach you how to live a lifestyle similar to theirs. I think of it as the wave in which the pandemic has taught us how to make money without leaving the comfort of your home.

My challenge to you as the reader of this book is to self-evaluate and explore how you see yourself and your personal relationship with money. Are you just like the young me that would let "money burn a hole in your pockets?". Or are you the older and wiser me that see money as a tool to gaining access for developing asset wealth through ownership? However you see yourself, maybe it is the hybrid of the two; you have to become realistic about what you want in life and what would it take financially to get there. In order to do that you must be conscious about how you save your money and what you purchase on a daily basis. The dollar you save today could be the same dollar you use to make a serious major purchase like homeownership.

Creating a savings is always important to have when it comes to purchasing a home. Some people have been able to bring 3.5% to the table as a down payment on a FHA loan. These loans typically have low closing costs. When I was studying to become a certified HUD counselor I learned so much about the different types of loans. Now there are many programs available to new home owners in the form of down payment assistance. A talented mortgage officer will have all of that information for you as you go through the loan process. Be sure to ask your loan officer about any programs that they have or know of for down payment assistance. Ask them if their company offers any down payment assistance programs? If they do not know any of this or don't even know what you are talking about it may be important to walk away and speak to someone else. See I also want to recommend that you interview different loan officers when you are going through the lending process. I also recommend this same strategy when you are searching for a real estate agent.

You have to know that when it comes to these types of professionals that you have options. And although you technically are not paying them upfront for their services, you must be reminded that they work for you. In that process the last thing you need to be mindful of is that you do not have to work with any agent that you do not like or have a hard time communicating with. These professionals are supposed to be nice so being nice and respected should not be the criterion to work with you that should be a given. You really should not focus on if they are nice to you. Your main objective is for them to be knowledgeable, motivated, savvy, and have a history of closing hard deals. I am not going to insinuate that your deal will be difficult because some deals are not. I am just saying that in the event that you do have any difficulty you need to make sure that you have a strong agent that is going to go to bat for you with underwriting and will communicate with you with information good, bad, or indifferent. You do not need a "yes man" when you are closing on a house.

    I remember my first agent on my first home purchase was very timid. I didn't understand at the time that she was new and her broker was calling all of the shots. Now trust me, I don't have any problems with new people in a profession having a learning curve, however, I do not want your learning curve with me. The broker knew I was ready to walk away from the deal, he felt it. One thing that I have learned throughout my professional career is knowing when it's okay to walk away from a deal that does not meet my full expectations. Especially when it comes down to how I spend my money. Let's be clear, yes they are lending you their money, however, once you sign the papers it then becomes your money so always be careful to be comfortable with any deal you're making that involves major purchases like homeownership. One thing that I knew early on that I would not do is purchase a home with an adjustable arm. What that means is the loan would adjust based on the market.

If you purchase a mortgage with an adjustable loan you could go from paying i.e. $900 a month to $1,200 a month. I am not willing to adjust my mortgages and play the market as if it's a lotto ticket. The only loans that I personally are ever comfortable with are Fixed interest rates. I do not like surprises like balloon payments in a set amount of years to come. We should play this asset development game as if we think the worst is coming and become surprised when the best presents itself. I like to know at all times what my payments are monthly so I can account for profits vs loss of properties that increase or decrease in value over the years. Saving up for down payment money is very important because it can in most cases "sweeten" the deal for getting you approved for a mortgage.

When clients approach me and ask for strategies on saving for down payment money I point them in the direction of pulling a set amount of money out of your bank account each month as if it's a bill. I have been paying magical bills for years that do not exist. These bills are just a fee that I debit out each month and it goes into a savings account. In most cases I do not see and think of it as building a bank account. I think of it as paying on a bill that will go towards a debt or "real bill" that I will pay to serve as a down payment on assets. Another strategy for down payment is asking your friends to gift you $1,000.00. I don't know what kind of friends that you have in your life but I stay connected with a group of people that make money for a living. If you have a friend in your life that does not have at least $1,000 is discretionary cash available then you may not be in really reliable company. I have been blessed to have people in my life that are really close to me that would offer their credit card or cash if they need it. I knew that it was time to get more people in my life that thought like me and gave like me when I fell off financially.

Most people will not admit when they fell off financially because they always want to appear as if they got it all together at all times. I have always been open about the rough times in my life where I lost everything. Yes that's right I lost everything three times in my life and came back. The only difference about the last time is I learned how to keep it with asset development. Asset development is a strategy that you use in business that will require that you work with a financial advisor to make sure you are in a position of possession. The position of possession teaches you that you always plan and live as if you are "going broke" however you advance as if you are "growing broke". I grow broke all of the time. One of the ways I grow broke is by not making frivolous purchases.

When it comes to purchasing something minor to major I tell myself I do not need it. In fact, in order to purchase something I tell myself to convince myself to purchase it. See when you do not have any addictions and lavish spending habits to prove to someone you would be surprised how much you save. In place of frivolous spending I use my discretionary capital to increase my assets and my whole life insurance policies. No I am not putting my money into death benefits, I am adding to my life benefits by increasing my policies each year.

Every year before my next birthday, I go over my assets that are tied into my insurance policies and increase and/or convert my term policies over to Whole Life policies. I also add additional IUL insurance policies. These are some strategies that have been in place for years thanks to my good friend Jon Sugick. Suge as we warmly called him before he passed, made sure he lived his life making sure people knew how important life insurance policies were. Not just for death but also in life. Suge said something to me that I would never forget. He said, "the greatest transfer of wealth is in life insurance".

Jon Sugic rest his soul, is the reason when I lost everything that last time, I made sure that I planned a strategy in building asset wealth through whole life policies. With that being said, if you have been blessed to have accessed information like this prior to the purchase of a house then you know that pulling from the cash value of your insurance policy or 401K can serve as a down payment. John was there for me when I needed guidance on how to get back on my feet. Having friends like John is very valuable. One thing about John is he would not let you fall if he called you friend. If he loved you and you were his friend you were a friend indeed. In deed also meant he had that $1,000 if you needed it so you can get back in the game. I am not saying get rid of your broke friends. I am saying evaluate your network because as we say in business, your network becomes your net worth. Here is an exercise I always do with people in my training and it sparks a thought provoking conversation every time.

Take out a pen and write down the names of the people in your life you speak to everyday. This could be close family or friends or both. Now next to their names write down their approximate yearly income. Now divide that income by 5 and see what number you come up with. Now compare that yearly income with what you make every day. In comparing these numbers ask yourself this. Do you need to bring your income above that number or are you happy with that income? Are you doing everything you can to increase your income? Do you know how to increase your income? Are you willing to increase your income? I ask that last question because I want you to be honest about your asset wealth development journey.

Some people are honest and say that they do not want to do anything different however they do want to make more money. These are the people that play the lottery each day and await a big payoff so they can be rich. Now I do not knock anyone's thought process on that because who am I to say that it cannot happen to them. I am just saying that it's been "sexy" lately to talk about business. I mean as a business developer there are people wanting to run business ideas through me all the time. I can respect that because I absolutely respect the interest in becoming a businessman or businesswoman. However, there are times that people try to engage me and mention that they want to start a business. When I ask what type of business you are interested in it's not uncommon to hear ,"Oh I don't know…I was thinking about getting into "real estate."

Now that's another sexy topic: real estate. I mean it should be sexy, it earned that title rightfully! What better way to build asset wealth than with real estate. The foul on the play for the "sexy real estate talk" comes when the person has not taken out the time to learn about ways to make money or start a business in real estate. Then I think they are going to wear my ear out learning when they can purchase some of these real estate gurus that sell courses. No...we are not doing that. I want you to learn how to be serious enough about a business that you take it serious enough to learn something about it. So when you do have an intelligent conversation about a topic such as real estate you can have more to say about it than,"how does real estate go?"

In my last book Acid Reflux I mentioned that my sister says you always have to "have a dog in the fight", meaning know enough about a topic that will engage a person to have another conversation with you later. Now for those of you who are serious about adding additional income to your personal finances you have to know that real estate is one of the fastest ways to go. I have made the quickest money in real estate through wholesaling property. It's not uncommon for wholesalers to pick up an extra $8,000 - $12,000 a quarter by just being the person that finds the seller and engage the investor in the purchase of the property. Who couldn't use an additional $32,000 - $48,000 a year for business income? You can set up a Limited Liability Company (LLC), open a business bank account, and open a business phone line to start your business.

When you times those efforts by two years your business can be bringing in an additional $64,000 - $96,000 to report as business income to your mortgage lender. If you look at a mortgage calculator and put in the numbers of your annual income and business income you can get an idea of what you can afford. This includes your credit score being above 700 and your debt to income ratio being under 43%. This is the recipe for success in securing a home for your future. I hope you know how important your future really is. I am often reminded of the people that I assisted with the purchase of their new homes last year and their fight for homeownership. One couple that I worked with brought tears to my eyes to think of how a new home improved their relationship and their lifestyle with them as a family.

Prior to the purchase of their home they were living in an area that was always ringing with gunshots and drive bys. They were renting and paying for parking each month for both of their cars. The thing that made me so proud of them is when they were teaching their son how to ride a bike for the first time. The reason he didn't know how to ride a bike yet is that they were afraid to be outside in their neighborhood. So the kid never had a chance to play outside. Once they moved into a new neighborhood their children were able to be outside a lot more and safely. Another thought about this couple is they never thought they could see the "American Dream" of homeownership because they didn't think they qualified or made enough income for homeownership.

They both worked and been on the same job for many years. What bothered me during this journey to homeownership is that they could not see themselves owning a home. They were cooperative throughout the entire process yet they were not hopeful about the approval process. During the process of going through underwriting they were both on pins and needles just waiting for the hammer to drop and tell them they were declined for the loan. I remember the morning of the closing even after they were approved. This beautiful family was nervous. They were skeptical about the approval all the way up throughout the end of the signing of the loan papers.

They were waiting any minute for someone to interrupt them signing documents to tell them that there had been a mistake and they were declined for the loan. After the paperwork was signed and the keys were handed to them they felt too numb to be excited. As you would guess, they assumed that someone would meet them outside and tell them to go back inside to return the keys to their new home. This experience is all too familiar for new homeowners. This is a feeling that a lot of new homeowners feel when they are really becoming homeowners. One of the things that really helped this couple to get through this process was the support of having someone they trust with them throughout the process.

This was to hold their hand and encourage them to take baby steps towards me just as a toddler does when he or she is walking toward momma for the first time. The steps are shaking but pogressive and the next thing you know that baby is running and jumping to both momma and daddy. That's how it is for homeownership as we work to create an environment that normalizes homeownership in black and brown communities. These communities of minorities need support, assurance, guidance, feedback, and a listening ear of their concerns. Just as we listen to their dreams, we also need to be available to listen to their fears. Having social support from friends and family is something that can be important for new home buyers.

I am not just talking about someone who can gift you $1,000 for your home but someone who celebrates and supports you in getting your home and you do the same for them. Last year during the pandemic I spoke on a panel that discussed social emotional learning. Social Emotional Learning (SEL) is something you're supposed to learn at an early age. In fact, according to Google social emotional learning is a methodology that helps students of all ages to better comprehend their emotions, to feel those emotions fully, and demonstrate empathy for others. These are things that you should learn as a child and it should advance as you become an adult. To go deeper into SEL we know that it is a process through which children and adults acquire and effectively apply the knowledge, attitudes, and skills necessary to understand and manage emotions. These set emotions should navigate towards positive goals so one can feel and show empathy for others in order to establish and maintain positive relationships and to make responsible decisions.

Unfortunately not everyone matures in this area therefore they become adults who can't fully grasp empathy and sharing economies. So with this in mind, we carry a false sense of burden for others that doesn't evolve certain people into the full "thought understanding" of working together for common goals. An example of working together can best be described in circumstances of creating social capital. Social Capital for me is best described as a network with similar values that create an inter-connected bond for the purpose of organizing to enrich and enhance each other. Social apital as it relates to increasing homeownership for black and brown communities should look like this. The creation of an information community that works to create a program that engages black and brown communities to introduce them to asset wealth processes.

The engine of this process would begin with a data driven tool that would collect information and analyse this information in order to create programming specific to this community's needs as it relates to homeownership. We have to be proactive about the problem so we can become reactive about the solutions. It's not enough to promote "buying up the block" programs. We have to be introductory about the idea that the block is being taken away from them because they are not aware of the full benefits of ownership and how it relates to asset wealth. Wealth is a scary word for some black and brown communities. The word for them can feel excluding and out of touch from their reality. We need to enhance our relationships with these minority communities so they know without any hesitation that social capital should and will include them. Now when we speak about social capital we draw from the exposure to the topic that people need social support from family and friends. But if they don't have access to supportive families and friends then the social capital community serves to be just that for them. This social capital community becomes the hands that reach out to the toddler that is walking towards them in the journey of homeownership.

Let's go a step further as it relates to the funding of this social capital community of homeowners. Let's talk about communities that set up a model that borrows from the business model of Grameen Bank. Grameen Bank is a microfinance organization and community development bank founded in Bangladesh. It makes small loans to the impoverished without requiring collateral. The only thing different is it would not be a loan, it would be a gift.

For example if 50 people were working together to purchase a home and each one gifted each other a set amount of funds for each other's down payment then this would be an example of providing support to increase homeownership for black and brown communities. This may not be the total answer but it is just a suggestion and talking point of what we can do as a community to increase ownership and shorten the wealth gaps in this country.

Chapter 4:

Jack and Jill Went Up The Hill

"If your business, agency, or organization works with people from poverty, only a deeper understanding of their challenges and strengths will help you partner with them to create opportunities for success".

- Ruby Payne

In the world of business the driving force behind advertisement is market research. It is the information that the researcher uses to create products and services that you purchase. We tend to purchase things in which we can relate to. If your parents always purchased new cars and clothes then you grow to experience these things as part of your value system, and heritage. However, in circumstances of generational poverty, people who grow up in a family in which there was a limitation to transportation, clothes, and even shelter will tend to value the things that they can relate to. These things of value may include relationships, food, access to possessions and standing up for themselves.

According to the Ruby Payne study, in families with generational poverty people are valued as possessions therefore the relationship with each other becomes highly valuable no matter how toxic that relationship is. This is just a small example of how people living from generations of poverty have passed down poverty mindsets that are targeted by capitalists who seek to benefit from this type of thinking. The marketing is towards these consumers that come from generational poverty. These consumers are triggered by advertisements and marketing that suggests that you deserve the product or services that they are offering.

For example, and I will not say the name of this automotive company. If you watch television commercials you can see how these high end automotive companies have created commercials using African American celebrities to entice the minority consumer to purchase this car or SUV. The black or brown consumer can relate to that celebrity because they have seen them on television over and over again. This person becomes relatable to the product or service no matter if they can afford it or not. The name of the game is not can you afford the car or SUV but more so can you see yourself driving the SUV; it doesn't matter if you have a great credit score for it or not. When it comes to homeownership we do not often see the relatability to ownership and why it is important. One thing about relationships is, it's just that. If you break down the words as my friend Tiffany would say, you can break down the meaning behind every word you speak.

For example, you do not have a relationship if you and another person can not relate. Furthermore, to ship is to move forward, so if we can not relate you surely can not ship or move forward. Therefore how can you move forward with the purchase of the product or service if there is no relationship, no ability to relate, and no ability to move forward. In order to sell to a customer you have to make sure that they can relate therefore you have to build a relationship with them. In building a relationship with your customer, who can we depend on to make sure that the customer has an understanding of the transaction? I am talking about the understanding to identify indeed if the stated transaction between the customer and the client is mutually beneficial.

The client needs a house and if you are the seller then you need the sale. Will the seller care if the consumer credit is bad and the transaction is costing the buyer an incredible amount of interest to purchase it? Nope. They will not even ask. They just want to know if you qualify to purchase and if not they are moving on to the next buyer. You are the one that needs to know and understand to what extent, of what you want, is costing you. So when we talk about the value system of a person that comes from generational poverty that person does not value credit scores and affordability. This person values that the person that sold this home to him was nice and they really wanted you to have that house. It was the personality and the relationship of the seller that sold the house. So being treated well by the seller served as a value of the transaction because the relationship was established for the deal.

This relationship value became more important than the consumer barely meeting the requirements to purchase it. You can talk to anyone that is in the industry of wholesaling property and they will tell you that a high percentage of their transactional income was derived because they were able to build a relationship with the buyer. That transaction is made whole because they were able to sell that contract with the original seller to an investor buyer. As a seller it is in your best interest to build a relationship with the buyer and be extremely nice. So guess what, the seller is supposed to be nice and you are supposed to know before you walk into the transaction if you can afford it. That is your responsibility as a consumer to know how to make responsible purchases.

So, if Ruby Payne is right then we are all in trouble. We are in trouble as a human race because there is so much work to do. Who is going to do the footwork of understanding poverty mindsets in order to better understand our relationship with money? If they are not doing it then we have to do it individually ourselves. Let's self-evaluate our relationship with money and our spending so we do not have to continuously live in a place of, I hope I can qualify for a house or a car. I want you to be in a position to experience that money does grow on trees. You just need to know what to plant in "fertile financial soil" so you can grow your money in your bank account just as grow money on our trees.

In order to make sure you are planting in "fertile financial soil" we often need to hear scenarios and real life cases so you can hear them, relate, and grow. For the purpose of this discussion, I am going to describe real circumstances, identify the problem, and present the solutions. The characters in these discussions will be called Jack and Jill. We will explore what it is like for Jack and Jill to get up the hill.

Jack is in his mid to late 50's, blue collar worker, with no children. Well at least no children that he is financially responsible for. His annual income is $70,000 and he has been working for the school district in transportation for over nine years. Jack owns two Mercedes Benz automobiles and his credit score is low 600's. Also, Jack has not filed tax returns in the last four years. Jack has never owned a home and continues to pay for a three bedroom apartment for $1,400 a month. Now Jack has thought about getting a home but has not thought about when and where he would like to purchase one. Well when you dig into Jack's background you will find that Jack's mother and father have never owned a house.

Jack's mother is almost 70 years old and has always been a renter. Jack's father has a similar backstory to his mom. Jack's grandmother or grandfather has never owned one as well. According to national standards Jack's mother was not necessarily what you deem as living in generational poverty. She worked a really good job over the years however, never made strides to purchase a home. Jack is not what you would consider as someone living in poverty. He makes well over the income line for poverty and low-income in the U.S. However, there are cases in which situational poverty can create low financial emotional intelligence. If we can't increase the financial emotional intelligence in Jack it's going to be a challenge in engaging him in understanding the push and purpose to purchase a home.

If you speak with Jack he doesn't seem too bothered about having a better lifestyle. His day to day actions include working 5 to 6 days a week and often taking on offered overtime hours. He wakes up at 5:30 am to get to work by 7:30 am. He works until 4pm and comes home and makes himself dinner. He may run a few errands that day, but soon comes home and plays a few hours of video games and gets ready to start his day over.

On his days off, he may go shopping and buy himself some expensive name brand clothes and other high ticket items. He has luxury automobiles that he brags about with his friends in front of his apartment home. He is the guy to look up to with these cars, clothes, and technology toys. Let's be real, we all know the Jacks in our lives. They are families, they are our friends. Heck, let's be real, we may be married to one.

The point I am making is if Jack is comfortable than Jack is going to spend the rest of his life spending his money the way he wants to unless Jack is introduced and accepts something different. I wonder if Jack can imagine himself with a house that is almost paid for because he has several rental properties that he owns. I wonder how close we could get Jack to imagining that he could realistically be able to retire shortly and debt free. Here are the problems that Jack would need to resolve in order to be able to get himself in a position to own a home, live debt-free, and retire early. The first thing we need to do is increase Jack's emotional intelligence. In order to help Jack increase his EI he needs to carve out about one hour a day reading. Reading and listening to audiobooks is one of the best ways to improve your personal and professional mindset.

Jack could also listen to different podcasts so he can get an opportunity to relate to what it is like living a different lifestyle that he is in control of creating. The best way to create a lifestyle is to read magazines and watch things that uplift and motivate you to live better and find a higher outlook on life and the lifestyle you want. Maybe you won't travel abroad to Bora Bora or sleep outside on a camping ground in Wyoming but you do owe it to yourself to see yourself wanting to achieve more. How often do you see people using their last money with no savings to take a cruise or go on an exotic vacation? It happens more often than you can imagine because most people are not going to tell you they scraped up their last penny to go on their vacation. What you will see on social media is beautiful pictures and poses in front of fancy hotel rooms and luxury cars and exotic exclusive beach scenes.

You won't see the times that they will call up their financial life raft to borrow money or ask for them to do a favor on credit. They won't post on social media the sob stories about being close to eviction and they don't know what they are going to do. Okay who am I kidding, yes sometimes they will still post their personal business of their needs. They don't seem to remember the photos that were taken less than a month ago that showed them living life on a rented jet ski, having a margarita looking out over the coast of Costa Rica. Low financial emotional intelligence in some consumers is how marketing continues its capital gains. They take advantage of these types of consumers that do not want to focus on the responsibility of money management. What's the fun in money management? Some people like Jack want to actually enjoy their life like this and really could afford to do so from time to time while making $70,000 a year. But not Jack, he spends his money elsewhere but not quite sure where. So to help Jack is to help him to increase his emotional intelligence so he can learn how to self-evaluate himself and prioritize his values.

The next thing we have to do to help Jack is to get a picture of his finances as it relates to income coming in versus going out. There are a lot of really good tools that Jack can use to track his income and expenses. These same tools will monitor his credit scores and give him suggestions on how to improve his credit. Jack is not without tools and resources, he is just lacking the emotional structure to pursue alternative options for a better lifestyle through homeownership. The ability for Jack to own means that he is the first in his entire generation to own a house. This places Jack in position to increase his asset wealth and balance his life for the better. With a low credit score like 600,

Jack is losing so much money monthly on high credit card interest rates. Well, not just on the credit cards but on the two high interest rate luxury end automobiles. By the way, both of those two high end vehicles are older models therefore he spends a lot of money on repairs and insurance for them. This can create added costs and not to mention, Jack can only drive one car at a time. Now I am not throwing shade on Jack and his wants of having two high end automobiles. I am just asking Jack to consider working on his credit to improve his scores to over 700, so maybe he can purchase two new models that he can park at his new home versus a rented apartment with public parking. No matter what Jack decides to do I just want Jack to be in the best financial situation so he can have a more enjoyable lifestyle than he currently has. No I'm not done with Jack here's a few more problems I want to identify for him.

These are the things that he needs in order for him to qualify for a new home if that's what he decides to do. One important thing that Jack is going to need to do is file his taxes. The new home qualification will need at least two years of filed tax returns. If he owes any taxes from previous years he has to make sure he has paid them. Some lenders will consider approving you for a loan if there is a payment plan in place with the IRS. Jack is not the only one in the world struggling to improve his lifestyle. He only needs to make a few adjustments in his life so he can be on the right path to homeownership and so much more. Jack income is not the problem in this situation, Jack needs to be more disciplined in his discretionary spending. Jack could also benefit from speaking with a financial advisor to help him with strategies for retirement plans. I highly recommend that you start that process sooner than later. With strategies in place that use infinite banking concepts or debt snowball methods you can pay your debts off earlier. Building asset wealth through homeownership can help you maximize your dollars so you can live a debt-free life and lifestyle of wealth development.

Now that we have Jack ready to climb the hill let's take a look at Jill. Jill is early 40's and has three kids ages 7, 15, and 24. Jill works as a professor and a freelance photographer with high end clients. Jill owns a modest SUV making payments in the amount of $400 a month. Her credit score is 690 and she has multiple credit cards with high balances. Jill is a renter paying $2,500 a month for a 5 bedroom house that she rents from a friend. She loves to take mini vacations often and does quite a bit of shopping each month online. She makes $42,000 a year as a professor and about another $21,000 a year as a 1099 contractor.

Jill grew up in a house owned by her mother until they lost the house when she was 19 years old. By the time they lost the family house Jill was in college and headed towards her career in arts and entertainment. Situational poverty occurred when her mom lost her employment and could not maintain the payments in the home and it went into foreclosure. This was a very horrible experience in the family at the time, and what it did psychologically for Jill is make her not ever think about purchasing a home. She doesn't want to make the same mistake that her mother makes with buying a home and losing income and potentially losing the home. So Jill would like to play it emotionally safe and not share in the disappointment by not attaching herself to the responsibility of owning a home. She would never want to take her kids through the psychological scars that she had as she experienced her mom losing the family home.

Her dad was not around so there was no "financial savior" with income that could support keeping the home. Jill too is a single mom so she believes that she would mirror her mom's circumstances if she was to lose her photography income or even her income as a professor. Job security is scarce so Jill likes to play it safe as if she could handle the eviction differently than she would a foreclosure. The truth is that there are so many financial resources in place to prevent a home foreclosure. Now we know that there are also a lot of resources in place as well for renters that need rental assistance. However, if you do not find those resources in 30 days you can be evicted immediately versus with foreclosures in most cases you have six months.

There are things you can do as a homeowner to qualify for mortgage assistance programs. I believe that there are a lot of renters like Jill that do not want to own a home because they fear that they will foreclose and lose their homes due to situational poverty. This could be true however, it is important to know that some states have judicial processes while some have non-judicial processes for foreclosure and depending on the state there is typically time to avoid losing the house so you can build income and stay in your home. The problem is Jill is afraid of the unknown. One of the things Jill can do is research programs that can help you keep your home in event she was to fall behind on payments. Although she doesn't own a house yet, it is beneficial to address the thing that inhibits you from wanting to consider homeownership. Jill is paying her landlord's mortgage every month therefore increasing the landlord's wealth assets.

The landlord has used some of the self-help strategies we talked about with Jack and created some extra income for himself. Jill has to make ontime payments to the landlord or the landlord will evict Jill right away. The landlord is not a cruel person, it's just the mortgage on that house is due every month and when Jill pays rent, the landlord pays the mortgage and then drops about $1,000 in his savings account each month. The landlord knows that scared money doesn't make any money. However, we wish in this scenario that Jill understood that scared money pays more costs than it should. Jill's fear of situational poverty has lowered her financial emotional intelligence.

Jill needs to be engaged by more single mothers who have purchased homes. She needs to increase her relationship with others who have been and currently in her situation so they can support each other through. Jill loves to meet new people and learn new things. One of the things she could benefit from is a workshop that discusses how you can use both w2 income and 1099 income as a business owner to qualify for a house that would cost less than what she is paying now. Jill needs to imagine what it would be like if she could pay $1,500 a month for the same amount of space she is renting now.

Jill, just like Jack, could benefit from using a tool that would track monthly income and expenses in addition to monitoring her credit profiles. This product would also give her suggestions on what she could do to increase her credit score to over 700 so she can qualify for a new home with a great interest rate. Jill, just as Jack did, can get up the hill with those children and build a legacy of Wealth Asset that she can leave behind to those kids debt free. Of course she would have to curb that obsession for extra online spending and excessive mini-vacations. She can then enjoy a home that she owns and maybe one day purchase a second home that she can rent out for extra income each month; she could then afford to have more vacations and do more shopping online within reason.

Jack and Jill are not bad people. They just have poor habits that come from having low financial emotional intelligence. Jack and Jill are no different from the others that we know in our lives. No one is making fun of them or poking holes in their deficiencies. The purpose of these examples is to make you more aware of the situations that can occur that would create barriers for attaining homeownership. I know that money can be a very emotional topic and it's so hard to do the things you need to do when you don't have it. Learning how to make money is a tough subject, however training your emotions to learn how to keep it is another. The good news is that people do not have to do it alone. There are tons of financial management resources available that you can use to track spending and just as many lessons on how to invest it. Just remember it's okay to ask for help when it comes to managing your personal finances.

"Once we find the edges of our personal puzzles and put them in place, it's going to be a lot easier to put the rest of the puzzle together to create the full picture of the life we want for ourselves".

– Dr. Tori Brown

Chapter 5:

Building an Ark With Homeownership

According to the Goldman Sachs research report it states that the fastest way to accelerate change and to effectively begin to address the racial wealth gap is to listen and invest in black women. As a black woman myself I can agree with that research finding. To be heard enough and to be considered as valuable enough to invest in is an "American Dream'. When I hear this it goes unnoticed that I often feel sidetracked for the many years that we haven't been heard in this country. Not as an American and not as a Black American or not even as a young or elderly Black American. See there are many voices to become represented in what would be heard by us. I think of the elderly Black American that was seen on the news the other day. She was in the middle of being foreclosed on for non-payment of mortgage.

She worked part-time prior to the pandemic at Walmart and she was well into her 70's. She was frail and weak due to her battle with illnesses but still determined to speak to the news reporter to tell her story. She is facing foreclosure on a house that she has owned for decades. She actually has more equity in the house than what's owed on the house. Unsure how to pay the $18,000 they were asking her for to keep the house she told the news that all she owned was in that home behind her. Her story is no different from others her age and to be honest her color. This situation unfortunately isn't just a black or brown issue but it's a situational poverty issue. As we know situational poverty does not have any color on it. However for this Black elderly lady she was losing a battle and giving her last ditch effort to be heard.

I prayed that someone out there heard her and could step in and be a voice and a support for her during this time. One thing I think of about this situation is how can we close the wealth gap between black and white if our elderly are continuously losing the property that they do own. My answer to this is we have to create a generation that can step in for the Grandmother or Grandfather or eldely aunt and uncle to purchase the property for them. We can't sit by and wait for anyone to save our families and communities other than ourselves. This is going to involve building a generation that is serious about building and preserving a generation that has been there for them.

These elders are the pillars of our communities. Many have raised their grandchildren when the parents were not available. The grandchildren must be introduced to ownership early so they can have a mindset of building community versus one that may tear it down. According to the Goldman Sachs report, "Imagine Black women closing the 90% wealth gap their households face compared to white households". I can imagine that only in the same breath can I imagine that for elderly black women. Not only can I imagine it for black women but I can see it if only, done with elderly black women in mind. I can see empowering these black women to reach back to empower the elderly black women to create self-sustainability for the aging populations of African Americans.

Building an ark with homeownership is Noah's blueprint for getting us ready for recessions. I'm not sure if you are noticing but the price of food is going up right besides the cost of gasoline and energy bills. The more you pay for household goods the more you realize that money needs to grow on trees. I mean face it, the cost of living is going to go up so your ability to spend on unnecessary stuff may need to go down. If you are a renter it's more than likely you are supporting your local business professional's rental company business. Your monthly rent row is going towards their mortgage and they are increasing the equity in their property.

The most difficult thing about that and what could happen can be even scarier. It happened back in 2008 when the housing market tanked. Some landlords could not afford to keep up the mortgage on the property so although the renter was paying the rent each month, the landlord wasnt always paying the mortgage. Ultimately that means that the foreclosure note is placed on the doors and the landlord then may get in the wind. So when the filings drop into the court systems and the eviction is ordered, the honest, hardworking, rent paying family is out on the street looking for shelter to rent. This is not uncommon and definitely not an old horror story to get you worried. I am just sharing something that could likely happen to anyone black or white. I am saying this to encourage choosing to explore opportunities to purchase a home that you own and as long as you pay you do not have to leave.

So I know I heard people say that they just do not want the responsibility of ownership. The responsibility of ownership is no different than the responsibility of growing up and taking responsibility to creating a stronger lifestyle and safe haven. This is part of the process of building an ark with homeownership. The act of ownership allows you to have something in your name of value that can grow over the years. According to the Center of American Progress, "In 2020, millions of households, especially African American and Latino households, faced unemployment and multiple health emergencies more or less from one day to the next. Yet many of these same households had few or no emergency savings to fall back on during this time." In most cases these populations could not come up with $400 for an emergency. According to their research "for example, in 2020, 46.7 percent of unemployed white households could not come up with $400 in an emergency, while 65.2 percent of unemployed Black households lacked access to $400 in such situations".

One of the ways that would have been helpful for these populations is if they had better credit histories. During the pandemic credit unions like Navy Federal were offering up to $5,000 personal loans to help people get through emergencies during the pandemic. One of the requirements for this emergency loan was to have satisfactory credit. Having a satisfactory credit history can help you prepare as you build a financial ark. As discussed previously, there are so many things that require satisfactory credit. This includes the purchase of a car, insurance, utilities, and access to purchase housing. We have to become cautious and serious about what we do with our credit and spending. Never take your last money to go on a YOLO (You only live once) trip, it's just not wise, especially right now while we are still in recovery from a pandemic.

It's not enough to talk about the wealth gap but we have to be consistent and deliberate with our intentions to make sure we stay on path with our goals to increase our lifestyle. Taking an entire year off from work helped me to manage my appetite for spending. Over the last year and a half of the pandemic I have dressed in T shirts and shorts even in my zoom meetings. I have refrained from using chemicals in my hair from beauty shops and maintained my own hair care. Last year I taught myself how to do so many things such as pedicures and manicures. I have been absent from expensive Seafood Dinners on the beach and waterfront of Tampa and replaced it with homemade recipes that I really enjoyed preparing.

It has been great connecting with people via Zoom that suddenly had time to converse about patents, inventions, investment properties, and cryptocurrency. I learned how to become a certified bartender and mixologist while taking classes on Udemy for editing video with Final Cut Pro. Not to mention catching up on reading, watching updated episodes of the hit television show Billions, and soaking up social documentaries on Netflix. Having this time to grow during the pandemic allowed me to save money and run up on some interesting ways to make money while staying in the comfort of your home.

Out of everything completed over this year of being off I am most proud of choosing to do what I wanted to do while I was "off the grid". I helped 47 people become homeowners and I worked with my board of directors to get ready to launch a non-profit that would design technology that would collect data for homeownership and create a community for black and brown homeowners. This technology is an App and a tool for engaging our social capital community. We want to heighten through this App a process that would increase more black and brown homeowners to decrease the wealth gap.

This tool would encourage satisfactory credit, money management, prompt fiscal responsibility, asset development, the power of ownership, and connection between the people and the professionals that are chosen to help our community become homeowners. Building an ark with homeownership takes a community. That community needs to be aware that someone is keeping them in mind as services and products are being created for them. This App is a resource for dealing with the mindset that goes with ownership and responsibility. According to the Ruby Payne Study systems have to be mindful of the population that comes from the systemic background of generational poverty. Not to say everyone of color has experienced it, but we can't be so careless to assume that a majority of the population of black and brown communities has faced generational poverty if not situational poverty.

Our goal is not to assume that they have or have not experienced poverty but to advance our discussion around the idea that resources for one group of people may not necessarily cater to another group of people. This is similar to the saying of "what's good for the goose, is good enough for the gander". Well who is going to stand up for the gander? The gander should not have to be subjected to something just because the goose was put in a position to become subjected to it. Different populations require different modalities of treatment. We know this in the field of medicine just as well as we do in the field of psychology. When you build an ark with homeownership you start with your first asset. Then you can grow into the purchase of investment property. From there you take the profits from your company of your investment property and build company assets though life insurance called key man policies. As these all grow you can work with a financial planner to place some of your profits into investments.

As you build your real estate portfolio you increase your company profits. One of the things that you can do is invest your money into opportunity zones in your state and community. These are special pots of money you can invest in property that are in specific locations called opportunity zones. These opportunity zones create great investment benefits that your company can use to grow asset wealth. The best way to do this is to build a support system and team of you all that's during the same thing at the same time. This act of social capital is what they call opportunities to "buy back the block", or anything else you can organize to compile your pool of money. Like I stated before, building assets is not easy, but indeed it is not that difficult either. While being mindful of your journey to building asset wealth; you do realize that you also can also use the concept of being mindful of building the ark with homeownership as a step in building stability for you and your family.

"I never thought about technology until technology thought about me. Artificial Intelligence (AI) seems to me to be thoughtful, engaging, helpful, and most importantly listening for the right information. We have a lot we can learn from AI. We should be listening before we ever choose to speak".

– *Dr. Tori Brown*

Chapter 6:

Situational Generational Poverty Solutions (SGPS)

Sometimes I am still amazed at Alexa and my Google Assistant. I also can't forget the first time I met Siri. Her gentle voice was both reassuring and passive as if she was speaking to my psyche to say, "trust me with your day". I trusted Siri just as much as I trusted a new barber about to cut my hair for the first time. I guess Siri was going to have to "show me just as much as she could tell me". As time went on I trusted my AI to answer basic questions like, "Google what time is it?". Then it advanced to "Google read me a bedtime story". Then in heavy rotation of work I would holler, "Google set a timer for 4pm!". That was Google then came Alexa. She tells me when someone is at the door. She tells me that Amazon shipped my package, and she even tells me that it's time to turn the television on to my mom's favorite show. Alexa, Google Assistant, and Siri all have something in common. While I am using it day after day, it's all collecting data on me.

It's getting to know me so it will know how to help me. Well help me and sell me something that can help me. I don't mind that at all, it doesn't bother me. It doesn't bother me any more than when a salesperson comes out of nowhere and tells me where the sales are and tries to get me to purchase something I did not indicate that I need. It's all sold and AI is at the curb of telling you it's in the driver's seat with technology. Some people just can't get with that. Many may call it a sign that big brother is watching, I don't know maybe he is. If he is, can we really do anything about it other than talk about it and discuss on and on how we don't like it. I don't think the invasion of privacy is anything anyone should like, however, we are in a place where technology is everywhere. During the pandemic I had a chance to go into McDonalds to order at a kiosk. It was so weird telling a machine I wanted fresh fries and it responded with confirmation that my selection was received.

Talking about AI taking into account what I wanted as a customer. Imagine if we created systems that did the same thing for us as future homeowners. This would be great right, you tell the system your problems and in a matter of months your problem compiles with other future homeowners similar problems and then next thing you know, you have an email with the problem solved. That would be great and help us achieve solution focused methods for minimizing barriers for homeownership in black and brown communities. The Situational Generational Poverty Solutions (SGPS) is an app developed for Fresh Community Development Inc to collect, analyse, and create programming solutions for increasing homeownership in black and brown communities. One may ask how important is the collection of data for these populations.

There are two ways in which data is collected, quantitative and qualitative. Quantitative is usually collected as surveys with multiple choice answers so you can weigh the worth of the question to a quantitative data set when analyzed can identify trends and information about the data you are collecting. Qualitative is typically collected in the form of audible collection of stories and verbal information that can be analyzed for generalized data that indicates a trend or occurrence of the onset of data. I learned in my early statistics class in my PHD program that data tells the real story. It speaks with truth when the measurables are both reasonable and reliable.

I learned in my early years of operating my non-profit agency when I ran data for a national program that Republicans love Quantitative data and Democrats love Qualitative data. When I was presenting to State Representatives and public officials it was important to know their political party so I knew which type of data set to present to them. I love data because it tells us the truth when most people are sold on telling us lies or mis-information. But be careful because in the wrong hands data can be manipulated. That's when data becomes dangerous when it gets in the wrong hands because the hand that holds it doesn't want to be caught being wrong. For the purpose of SGPS the data collected will be used to empower. As a therapist and researcher it's my profession to explore the problems for the purpose of creating a solution. In psychology we were given an opportunity to learn solution focused modality of treatment.

I always liked this method because as a therapist it allowed me to quickly dig into the problem so I can spend the rest of the limited sessions focusing on the solutions. In cases of therapy of what we call managed care, we would be given a client with substance abuse issues and asked to get them well in eight sessions. That eight sessions of 50 minutes meetings and they are gone back to face the life they got in trouble with to get to me in the first place. So for resolution focused therapy was more efficient. With the short amount of time available to treat them I had session one to engage them, get to know them, get them comfortable enough to tell me the truth, and get to the bottom of the addiction. With this modality I could spend the next six sessions treating them and the last session to give them resources to keep them from ever coming to see me again.

My mentor always taught me that the sign of a good therapist is to do so well with my clients that I work myself right out of a job by not seeing the same clients twice in one year. I tried very hard to do that and when I practiced I did very well with my clients. I use the same methods here with the technology. I listen for the problem, identify a trend of the problem, create solutions for the problem, implement a program to address the problem, and get ready for the next problem. The main problem we are experiencing with homeownership overall is the lack of tools available for connecting the data with the problem then connecting the problem with the solution all in one app. Sure when I look online I see many mortgage companies that use expensive CRM and click funnels that ask you to enter your name and email address for pre-approvals for housing.

This is an attempt to connect the potential buyer with the resources to speak to a lender about the home buying process. In many cases this is a helpful system. However, when you are dealing with Black and Brown potential home buyers this can be an overwhelming process. This process can also be a deterrent to ignoring future emails sent regarding going forward in the process. The need for specialized services that integrate the collection of information to in turn provide information will engage this population. We all can use visual tools and community support through an app like SGPS. SGPS addresses both Situational and Generational Poverty with the focus of creating a solution for closing the gap by creating information based on the specific needs of the Black and Brown communities.

We have technology in everyone's hands via mobile phones. The text messaging system has been widely used throughout the world and advanced from communicating with characters to emojis to videos to confirming online sales purchases. These are the same systems we should be using in housing to communicate with our dear populations of black and brown mobile users. SGPS is currently in its alpha development stage and will go into beta before the end of 2021. The beta testing of this app is how we improve on our ability to successfully integrate technology with the home buying process. We believe in the importance of creating tools that directly connect the data collected with the information content delivered to the potential homebuyer for the sole purpose of connecting the buyer with the right agent to serve their needs.

Agents will benefit from this tool because SGPS will have done the psychosocial housing development social worker aspect of engaging the clients for the home buying process. This is the tough part of the process. Addressing the fears and uncertainty of the need for obtaining homeownership. How can we purchase something in which we do not have a reference point for having the need for it? We may not see the direct correlation of why we need it. Do we all need housing? I believe that we do. Do we all need homeownership? I believe that we do, however what I believe is not important over what black and brown communities believe that they need. What they need far exceeds what we believe that they need. We have to be responsible for asking the questions regarding what they believe that they need. How can we create a program for something in which we do not understand?

I am reminded of my work as young CEO of a non-profit organization in early 2005. I remember our organization being selected for several grant proposal submissions to work with underserved populations. When asked what was the secret to developing programming and writing the award winning grant my response was simple. I always listen to the population that my grant is targeting. How was I able to listen? I was always around the population that I was serving and engaging them continually to always hear them and understand their needs. I was always listening and collecting data from them and analyzing trends that spoke to me in clear context.

The programs developed were not written from a place in which I created because I felt that they needed it. It was written because I heard directly through the collection of data what they wanted and needed. SGPS is just as attentive as AI listens to the black and brown communities. SGPS will listen to the real estate agents and mortgage lenders. I have listened to my sister for years talk about how as a real estate agent people would reach out to her to sell them a house. She would take them around from house to house only to find out that they were not even pre-approved for a home and did not know what they needed to become pre-approved. She would then connect them with the referring mortgage lender and that lender, overwhelmed at times, asked the potential homebuyer for items that they didn't even have. By this time the person was overwhelmed and felt rejected and not ready for the process.

This in turn could discourage the buyer to avoid reviewing future options for homeownership. And to be totally honest the realtor was too overwhelmed to follow through with that buyer in fear that they were just a waste of time and it's literally another person looking to buy a home coming in right behind them. That person may be more prepared than the last person so this person becomes the person that the agent energy is focused on. As for the potential buyer they are stacking inquiries on their credit report for looking to become pre-approved for housing. It's so easy for our black and brown homebuyers to get lost between the cracks so SGPS is necessary.

SGPS has its advantages because the data will tell us what they need and the content will tell them what they need to prepare for the home buying process. Once they are participating in the social capital community presented in SGPS they will be able to identify their interest in homeownership and receive the process for obtaining it. Homeownership is an investment in self because it lends to the opportunity to own something that will benefit your family from generations to come. Poverty does exist however, it does not have to stay prevalent in our black and brown communities. We can use technology in a way in which it helps us to do our part in our communities, one data set at a time.

For more information on SGPS visit the website www.freshcommunitydevelopment.org or text "SGPS" to 1.888.697.0965.

EPILOGUE: ALL MY FAVORITE COLORS

"If there was ten white children hungry and ten black children hungry, I would figure out how to feed twenty hungry kids"

- Doc

I graduated with my undergraduate degree from Eastern Michigan University with a bachelor's degree in Psychology and African American Studies. The reason that I ended up graduating with a double bachelors is because after taking my first course with African American Studies and law professor Dr. Ronald Woods, my excitement to learn about my culture just couldn't stop. It became an addiction to continue to take these classes that did not exist in my K-12 Education. I was hungry and inquisitive taking class after class after class trying to find myself in my blackness. Growing up in Saginaw Michigan my educational experiences were pretty well rounded when it came to attending with diverse students from different cultural backgrounds.

In middle school I attended a school for "the gifted" called The Center for The Arts and Sciences (CAS). Walking the halls of that school was like taking a page from the hit television show Fame. Youth dancing in the halls, artists creating oil paintings everywhere, and math and science, the class I was invited to attend, we wore white lab coats. I thought the days of walking those halls would never end. I just knew the school year would take forever. That year I asked my mom if I could attend middle school full time again and leave CAS; she quickly rejected my request.

She thought it was good that I was integrated with other youth my age and older from different backgrounds and socioeconomic statuses. Where in the hell did she get those words "backgrounds", "socioeconomic" and "status" from? We didn't speak like that at home! It turned out these were the words the Assistant Principal of CAS passed on to her, to encourage me, to make the best out of my experiences at this school. It was a predominantly white and middle to upper class student body. After some tough persuasion, my mom finally at least let me change into another class they offered, Language Arts and Creative Writing. It was here that I was introduced to Shakespeare, Edger Allen Poe, and some other famous American writers that didn't look like me.

I really struggled to be in this class, not because I could not keep up with the workload, it's because I didn't want to keep up with the workload. I wanted to write what I wanted to write and the way that I wanted to write it. I often submitted for classwork, raps that I wrote that would describe my neighborhood but in the form of what I felt was poetry and my personal rendition of a prose. What is a Prose? A Prose is an ordinary language that follows regular grammatical conventions and does not contain a formal metrical structure. This definition of prose is an example of prose writing, as is most human conversation, textbooks, lectures, novels, short stories, fairy tales, newspaper articles, and essays. I'm sure that I drive my book editor and publisher crazy because I still continue to write my books and anything I compose as a personal rendition of a prose. In my PHD program, I am certain that my advisor Dr. Ellington was as frustrated by my rebellion on APA style writing. I accepted all of the criticisms and feedback during my dissertation but continued to write it the way I wanted to write it.

Even when I started my first non-profit organization writing hundreds of grants and contract proposals, writing became something that I was comfortable at doing because it allows me to communicate and enlighten. So growing up in a mixed population educational system it became natural for me to blend in and get to know different races, cultures, and classes. I really loved what I learned from my K-12 experiences because it assisted me in becoming who I am today. However, taking so many African American Studies classes so that I could double major in was just really great icing on the cake. Psychology in conjunction with African American Studies allowed me to explore various topics and research studies on communities and cultures. I wanted so badly to understand how the black side of town could have so many liquor stores and the white side of town didn't.

I was intrigued by how the only time we had white visitors at our church was when it was election time. I also at the same time wanted to understand the beautiful language that my neighbors spoke. They were a sweet and loving family that spoke Spanish and always had the best parties, music, and food. I wanted so badly to have an understanding of why the Brandy Bunch was always so happy on television. They had a lot of people in their house just like I did growing up with an eight household environment with one bathroom. My sister was nothing like Marsha and my brother with nothing like Greg. I wanted to learn more about how Mike Brady was an Architect and how he became one. That intrigued me because I too wanted to design houses. I knew that for sure when I did design houses, it would for sure have more than one bathroom in it. In fact, I told myself to "design houses so everyone who wanted to live like the Brady Bunch could" but at an affordable price.

It bothered me that when I would go to other people's homes and those homes didn't even look like the one I grew up in. I wasn't bothered because I judged them, I was bothered because I wanted them to live better. I wanted them to be in a nice clean home like I grew up in with no roaches, a working toilet, running water, backyard to play in, and good transportation to get around town. My parents never had to get a ride from others or borrow money from people. My parents were always the ones doing the lending. The people I grew up with often thought we were rich. I don't believe we were, I mean we ate daily and was blessed to have both mom and dad, however to be honest I think the biggest factor is my parents always had great credit.

They always had credit cards, cash, and Cadillacs. I understood early that if I was to continue to have a lifestyle of the big 3 (Credit Cards, Cash, and Cadillacs) then I had to attend college, purchase a house, and earn a living using my mind. My dad used to tell me all the time growing up that I needed to find a job sitting on my ass. This is partially because I always found effective ways to complete my house chores like washing dishes sitting in a chair in front of the kitchen sink or cooking. He thought that was so lazy and often discouraged it with loud "curse outs" and rants. Don't worry, out of all of the Zodiac signs I was the only earth sign in the household, everyone else are fire signs. So what that means is someone was always ranting, fussing, and on the verge of getting a "curse out".

I guess it plays to my advantage because I grew up with that type of behavior all around me. To this day and especially in relationships, I tend to block out people that do that. Franky, I don't care who gets mad because anger is something I believe that we are all entitled to. The line gets crossed in event that the situation gets physical then that becomes another type of situation. In Black life as we say it, there are some things that we experience that makes us who we are, especially if we are "keeping it 100". However, to keep it 1,000 when it comes to my culture, I want to do my part to normalize things like homeownership for people that look like me.

I think it's a lot of dope programs out here and tools that people like me can use to gain access to homeownership. But, these tools do not just operate on their own. We have to use them and be diligent about the use of them. Now I agree that there are some barriers that prevent people that look like me from becoming homeowners. Some of those barriers are built within our internal locus of control. According to Google, Locus of control is what an individual believes causes his or her experiences, and the factors to which that person attributes their successes or failures. People with a high internal locus of control believe that they are in control of their own success or failure; that success or failure is not the result of chance or fate.

An example of this is when I spoke with a cousin about buying a home. He has been on his same job for 7 years and he continues to stay a renter. When I asked why he has not purchased a house by now his response is, "these folks are not going to let me get a house". I am not going to play stupid right here and pretend as if I don't know whom these folks are that he is referring to, nor will I justify the statement by explaining who the folks are. Lets just call them for the sake of discussion "the influenced powers that be". I will leave you with the duty of describing for yourself, who the "powers" that he is referring to are. What I will say is he does not truly understand his true powers. He does not understand that with the right amount of income and the right credit score and the right amount of information to provide to lenders, he can too qualify for a home and begin the road to asset wealth and power, just like that.

However, his internal locus of control along with his external locus of control makes it difficult for him to believe in himself for his desired result of homeownership. This, in addition to the engagement continuance to believe that his luck just wouldn't allow it to happen for him. Homeownership is not luck or for certain people that are rich. It's for the people that are responsible and willing to make some changes in their spending habits so they can see the American Dream.

I love music and always have always will. I remember as a child, listening to John Cougar Mellencamp song "Little Pink Houses" and hearing the words…"There's a black man with a black cat living in a black neighborhood, he's got an interstate running through his front yard, you know he thinks he got it good"….then it goes on to the chorus "ain't that America for you and me? Home of the free, yeah little pink houses for you and me". In my perception, that song was addressing that homeownership is normal and attainable. It placed an early indicator in my mind that one day I would own a house. I guess my creativity also pictured John Cougar Mellencamp being my neighbor and he would play his guitar and dance just as he is portrayed on MTV in the 80's.

As I became older, it bothered me that this type of American Dream was not the case for so many others that looked like me. The older I become the more I realize that this is not even the case for a lot of people no matter what their race or color is. I realized that a locus of control can impact anyone at any time when it comes down to homeownership. Yes I believe that we need more resources and information to address the disparities of ownership and the wealth gap between black and white people. Yes I believe that we need more resources to increase homeownership in black and brown communities. I also believe that with the right information and right alignment of people, we can help more people black, white, yellow, and brown people become homeowners no matter their socioeconomic status. When I wrote this book I prayed for a book title that would speak to the depths of why I wrote this book.

My intent and desire in writing this book is to address some hard topics that most people do not want to address and will not address. But thanks to my upbringing around fire signs and great music, I tackled something that needed to be tackled daily. Inclusiveness and discussion. I am serious about increasing homeownership and the reason why I know this is true is because I wrote another book to share with you my expertise, expressions, and energy in dealing with increasing homeownership. I am serious about the ownership period rather than homes, businesses, equity positions, stocks, crypto, or intellectual property. Ownership of information is key and the unlocking of information is currency.

I wrote this entire book and a random song played on my Apple Music and I turned it up. Tears came to my eyes as the young man sang the most beautiful words ever heard. I knew when I heard it that this was going to be on repeat on my playlist. As I listened I couldn't help but think how beautiful of a topic this would be as I write about something so sensitive yet so dearest to me. He sang just how I felt about the world and the people in it that just want to be heard. It didn't help while I was listening to the song at the same time the news was in my background and I could hear the social media upset about humans being hit with whips at the borders.

All I could think of was my God! So many people need a place that they can call home and here we are with a home or an opportunity to purchase a home and we are not thinking just how blessed we are. Having an opportunity to get a home is a blessing and we have to see it as just that. As the song played my heart knew what I had to do and just how I had to do it. Rather I wrote it as Prose or Poetry, I knew it had to be written and for whom it had to be written for as the song sings," ...All my favorite colors, my sisters and my brothers, see them like no other, all my favorite colors…".

ABOUT THE AUTHOR AND FRESH COMMUNITY DEVELOPMENT INC

Dr. Tori Brown wears many hats when it comes to providing services to others in Tampa Bay and beyond. She has an extensive background in business development, learning, consulting, community, and non-profit organizations. The mission of Fresh Community Development Inc is to provide cost-effective resources to low-income families in need of financial and business literacy to improve their chances for access to housing or homeownership. She is leading a team of board of directors to do just that.

After assisting 47 families with becoming homeowners during an international pandemic, it was inevitable that the next steps would be to impact a larger community. Increasing homeownership in black and brown communities is a step in the direction of closing the wealth gap between black and white. The celebration of diversity is very important for Dr. Brown. Helping everyone have access to homeownership is the goal of the programs that she creates. Just as black, brown, and white exist; so does have and have not, poor, working poor, and living in poverty. We all have a role to play when it comes to coming together to fight the fists of poverty. This book The Color of Homeownership is just one of the tools. For more information on Dr. Tori Brown be sure to visit her official website www.DrToriBrown.com.

www.ingramcontent.com/pod-product-compliance
Lightning Source LLC
Chambersburg PA
CBHW071903070526
44583CB00016B/1824